Samuel Harris

Inaugural Address Delivered by Samuel Harris

At His Induction Into the Presidency of Bowdoin College, August 6, 1867

Samuel Harris

Inaugural Address Delivered by Samuel Harris
At His Induction Into the Presidency of Bowdoin College, August 6, 1867

ISBN/EAN: 9783337125530

Printed in Europe, USA, Canada, Australia, Japan

Cover: Foto ©Andreas Hilbeck / pixelio.de

More available books at **www.hansebooks.com**

INAUGURAL

ADDRESS

DELIVERED BY

SAMUEL HARRIS

AT HIS INDUCTION INTO

THE PRESIDENCY OF BOWDOIN COLLEGE,

August 6, 1867.

BRUNSWICK:

JOSEPH GRIFFIN.

1867.

At a meeting of the Association of the Alumni of Bowdoin College this day held, it was unanimously voted, that the Alumni present their thanks to President Harris for his very able and acceptable Inaugural Address, and request a copy for publication.

Also, that His Excellency Gov. Chamberlain, with Hon. Samuel P. Benson, and the Rev. J. O. Fiske, be a Committee to carry this vote into effect.

Attest,

J. B. SEWALL,

Secretary.

BRUNSWICK, AUG. 10, 1867.

REV. SAMUEL HARRIS, D.D.

PRESIDENT OF BOWDOIN COLLEGE.

DEAR SIR:

In compliance with the accompanying vote the undersigned have the honor to request a copy of your Inaugural Address for publication.

We trust that you will in this way allow a wider influence to that noble exposition of sound scholarship, the spirit of which is to characterize the College over which you are called to preside.

We are with high respect,

Your friends and servants,

J. L. CHAMBERLAIN,
SAMUEL P. BENSON,
JOHN O. FISKE.

BOWDOIN COLLEGE, AUG. 30, 1867.

GENTLEMEN:

I thank the Alumni for their kind reception of my Inaugural Address, and transmit a copy for publication.

With much respect,

Sincerely yours,

SAMUEL HARRIS.

His Excellency GOVERNOR CHAMBERLAIN,

Hon. S. P. BENSON,

Rev. J. O. FISKE,

Committee.

INAUGURAL ADDRESS.

It is a German legend that the emperor Charlemagne returns every spring to bless the German land. Up and down the Rhine he walks, flinging his blessing on gardens, vineyards and fields, to make the seed spring up and to multiply the vintage and harvest. The significance of the legend is realized in every anniversary of a well-ordered institution of learning. As the college sends out its successive classes of trained and cultivated minds, it is its venerated founders, benefactors, and supporters who reappear in the scenes of their life-long interest to fling their blessing on the land which they loved and served, to quicken every healthful growth, and to multiply the ingathering of human joy. The trust now committed to me I seem to receive, not merely from you who are now the supervisors of the College, but rather from the departed good who have given of their property for its endowment, or consecrated to it the loving and self-denying work of their lives. It is an admonition to faithfulness, a stimulus to endeavor, an incentive to courage, a pledge of success. An institution, which by its living growth has organized into its own being the faith and love, the prayers and benefactions, the self-denial and toil, of noble men for two generations, deserves to live, and is not likely to die. It deserves and will reward the like precious offerings in time to come.

The occasion determines my subject. I must speak of THE NECESSITY, THE IDEA AND THE METHODS OF COLLEGIATE EDUCATION.

I. *The necessity of collegiate education.*

There is a floating impression that the diffusion of knowledge is all that is needed in a Republic. Already enthusiastic editors have predicted a good time coming when books will no longer be published or read, and the newspaper will be the only and the sufficient literature.

But the fountains of knowledge must be full, or the streams will not flow. Diffusion presupposes concentration. It is easy to say that the fruitfulness of the earth depends on the general diffusion of moisture. But the moisture must first be condensed by the mountain tops and gathered into springs that feed the streams. Colleges are the mountain tops which fill the fountains whence knowledge is diffused.

Besides, science is different in kind from popular knowledge. For example, beneath the popular knowledge of Astronomy, Physics, Chemistry or Mineralogy lies hidden, like the skeleton within the body, a complicated frame-work of mathematics. Not only the *savans* who perpetuate and enlarge science, but the teachers and authors who diffuse it, and the professional men who apply it must have scientific as distinguished from popular education.

Men, also, of thoroughly trained intellects and of rich literary culture are indispensable to the welfare of society. The civilization which has ceased to produce them is already effete.

Without this liberal education, charlatanism and quackery will displace science and skill in the professions, the demagogue will usurp the place of the statesman, the disorganizer that of the philanthropic reformer, and instead of popular intelligence and the diffusion of useful knowledge, will gradually come in the diffusion of popular delusion and superstition.

Especially in this country thorough and complete collegiate education is needed to counteract the tendency to superficiality pervading and enfeebling American civilization.

It may not be unnecessary even to insist that colleges are congenial with a democracy. Side by side in the class-room sit the son of poverty and the son of wealth, the boy delicately and luxuriously reared and the sun-browned laborer, the youth of genteel and polished manners and the youth having no acquaintance with the graces. The conceit of one, the boorishness of another, the bashfulness of another are worn away. The one standard of reputation and influence is talent, scholarship and manly merit. There is no community more thoroughly democratic in its influences, or in which the determination of a man's standing is more free from factitious distinctions and tests.

But this is not all. Colleges are indispensable to democratic civilization. The culture incident to aristocratic birth is lacking. We cannot replace it with a coarse aristocracy of wealth. Then we must have instead the culture of thorough education.

The very rapidity of the national growth demands it. The rapid advance of population into the wilderness has created in the West a peculiar type of American civilization, characterized by rapidity of thought, strength of conviction and energy of action; but certainly not by thoroughness of education, breadth of knowledge, or richness of culture. Out of it have arisen politicians uneducated in the schools, but earnest and strong. Because a few of these have won public confidence, the people have been ready to jump to the conclusion that a lack of early and thorough education is a positive recommendation for high office. Time will teach us better. It will expose the narrowness, one-sidedness and incompleteness of half-educated men, however strong. It will demonstrate that even Western civilization, with all its daring and energy, cannot successfully override the universal law which demands thorough training, broad information and deep culture for the wise administration of affairs.

This higher education is also needed to quicken, guide and purify human progress. Our own history is an example. In the earlier period of Massachusetts and Connecticut colonies, it was ascertained that about one in every one hundred and fifty inhabitants was a graduate either of Oxford or Cambridge. The great reformations of the past originated with men trained in the Universities. Wickliffe was acknowledged to be "incomparable in scholastic studies." Huss at the age of twenty was professor in the University of Prague. Reuchlin at the same age taught philosophy, Greek and Latin at Basle. The others, who, like these, bear the sad but sublime title of "Reformers before the Reformation," were trained in the highest education of their time. Luther and the leaders of the Protestant reformation were "college-learned" men. Bilney, Tyndal, Fryth,—young men praying over their Greek Testaments at Cambridge and Oxford—conveyed the spiritual power of the Reformation to England. John Knox was a scholar and a teacher at St. Andrew's. The Puritan leaders need only be named to prove the indebtedness of that movement to the universities. Methodism originated in the highest seats of learning in Great Britain. Nothing can be more erroneous than the common assertion that reforms originate with the uneducated and work upward. History declares that the ideas and movements which transform the world have originated with men of the highest education, often be-

2

fore they had left the schools; that they have usually been proclaimed by such men before the people were ready to receive them, and often at the price of persecution and martyrdom. Thus it has been truly said, Tell me what some scholar is thinking in the solitude of his study today, and you tell me what in the next generation will be the watchword of progress and the staple of the hustings.

II. *The Idea of a College.*

The college, and the university in which the professional schools are included, imparting scientific education and liberal culture, must be distinguished from the common schools, and equally from each other. The precise idea of the college must be accurately determined in order to correct crude notions as to what its studies should be and what it may reasonably be expected to accomplish for its students.

The college is preparatory to the professional school. It aims to develop the man, to ground him in the principles of knowledge, and to make him acquainted with its methods and instruments. The professional school and the school of industry and arts, aim to impart the special training and knowledge necessary to a special profession.

On the one hand there must be the special education. Hippias the sophist taught that the object of education is to make a man sufficient for himself. He therefore appeared at the Olympic games boasting that all the articles of jewelry and clothing which he wore were manufactured by his own hand; at the same time he exhibited all sorts of poems, epic, tragic and lyric, and several kinds of prose composition. An attempt to educate a man to be sufficient for himself in this sense, would annihilate the division of labor and reduce society to barbarism.

On the other hand, as really disastrous would be an education imparting exclusively the special training and knowledge for a special art or profession.

The college, then, aims to effect a systematic and harmonious discipline of the whole man, and thus to prepare the student for the special study and training necessary to fit him for his special business in life. He is not shut up by his college education to one of the so called learned professions, but is trained as a man so as the more readily to master any business, and in whatever business to possess stronger powers, a better balanced mind, a richer culture, and a broader sympathy with all true minds and true learning in other professions.

This being the idea of a college, its prime and dominating end must be, not to impart knowledge, but to strengthen and discipline the mind, to put the man in possession of himself, and to enable him with the greatest facility to achieve the greatest and best results. It is not to bloat the man with a plethory of learning, leaving him flabby in organization, slow, feeble and awkward in movement; but to train him to the development of intellectual muscle, to quickness, power and dexterity in intellectual action.

First, physical culture must not be neglected. But here observe that it does not belong to the college to train the senses to the special uses, and the hand to the special dexterity necessary in special pursuits. Such training belongs to professional schools, to schools of the arts, and to apprenticeship to trades. Nor does it belong to the college to train men to the highest development of muscle, of agility or speed; for such training belongs only to the professional athlete and acrobat. This is an extraordinary training of special powers, incompatible with the full-orbed and harmonious development of the man, and unfavorable to the greatest health and longevity, and to the best intellectual advancement. No people ever gave more prominence to physical culture than the Greeks; yet Plato insists that the training of an athlete must not be permitted in the education of the young. He says that the athletes are intellectually a sluggish set, who doze away their lives, and that they are of dubious and unreliable health. He therefore insists that the gymnastic training of the young should be more simple and moderate, and recommends military drill.

Physical culture must also be kept in subordination to intellectual. If it absorbs the interest and energy that should be devoted to study, it frustrates its own design and makes the whole college course nugatory. There should be that degree and kind of physical culture which are essential to vigorous health; so as to insure the greatest serenity of spirit, capacity for work and power of endurance; so as to dispel despondency and gloom, exhaling like mists from the man's own disordered liver; so that he may not break down under the first strain accompanying the severer exigencies of life; so that it may be every day a joy to live and work. Other things being equal, the healthy man is the happiest and makes others the happiest; he is the more pleasant husband and father, the more generous friend, the cheerer and helper of the sad; in every position and relation the wholesome man. He radiates joy. Health, as the perpetual spring of animation and energy, is the first requisite of success. It must never be out of sight in the administration of a college.

The college must also train the intellect so as to give it both strength and dexterity. There are three kinds of intellectual power, *thought, expression, execution*. By the pre-eminence of one or the other of these the regal minds of the race are characterized. The college must train them all.

There is first the power of thought. Ordinary scholars may not enlarge the bounds of human knowledge by discovery, nor originate thoughts which the world will not willingly let die. But since they ought to be, in their respective spheres, the "*cardines rerum*" on which events and actions turn, they must be trained to original and independent thought—original in the only sense in which originality is possible to ordinary minds, that they have looked at things with their own eyes;—independent, because they do not receive their opinions from others but have thought out conclusions for themselves. They must be able to see the significance and bearing of events, look through appearances to reality, detect the errors of popular opinion, and be wise counsellors of the people. The first aim, then, is to make the student a thinker; to train him to attend fixedly and long, to observe, discriminate and define, to analyze, compare and combine, to weigh evidence and reach just conclusions; that his mind may be, not a warehouse filled with bales of facts, but a growing germ, organizing material into its own substance and force, as an acorn organizes the soil, water and air into a living oak.

The second kind of intellectual power is that of expression; the power of communicating, vindicating and enforcing thought. It is the power of the teacher, the orator and the author. The training of this power is the special object of one department of college instruction, and should not be overlooked in any. The study of language, though distinct from the department of rhetoric, is the study of the instrument of expression, giving that scientific knowledge of the history, significance and relations of words, and of the combinations and possibilities of language, which is an unseen but effective help to precision and power of speech. And every translation—and indeed recitations in other departments—should be an exercise in using simple, perspicuous, precise and terse language.

Next is the power of applying and combining thought in executive and administrative action. This is the power of the inventor, the reformer, the general, and the statesman ; also of the lawyer, physician and clergyman, using science, skill and training for the uses of daily life. This power must not be neglected. Philosophy formerly was contemplative and not active, withdrawing from action to academic shades and to retreats of learning. Barrow in his Greek Professorship called himself an "Attic owl driven out from the society of all other birds." But at this day and in America every scholar should be a worker. All thought is to be transformed into life. An education which makes a man only a book-worm, which unfits him for the activities of life, is a failure. The philosophy of America must be the Peripatetic. From the nature of the case, special training for special lines of business must be in the professional schools. But this grand obligation of every scholar to a life of action must control the whole college curriculum, so that the student acquire that facility in handling all his faculties and acquisitions, which will fit him to succeed in any line of action, industrial, military, political or professional.

Argument is superfluous to demonstrate that this is the result of a right college training, and of the training actually given at Bowdoin, since we are

honored with the presence of his Excellency the
Governor, distinguished at once as scholar, general
and statesman.

They, therefore, greatly mistake, who estimate the
value of the college course by the amount of learning
which it imparts; by the number of facts stored in
memory which the man can afterwards make use of
in his farm, workshop or office. Much more do they
mistake who suppose that the chief value of the four
years at college is in the opportunity for general reading and that acquaintance with English literature
which one can comfortably acquire in his easy chair.
It is the object of a college to make men. It is an
old and classic illustration, when you give a sheep
grass, you do not expect it to return grass, but wool.
So when you give a youth instruction you do not expect him to return learning, but manhood; not the
crude and undigested facts received, but a mind strong,
disciplined and dextrous in the use of all its powers,
and rich in culture.

I have spoken of physical and intellectual training.
But as physical training is subordinate to intellectual,
so both are subordinate to moral and spiritual ends.
The importance of this part of education has been
urged by the greatest educators and the greatest
minds in all ages. In reading the thoughts of the
Emperor M. A. Antoninus one is impressed by the
earnestness with which through nearly twenty open-
ing sections he enumerates the successive influences

which had established him in various moral principles and expresses his gratitude for them. Plato in his system of education for his model republic dwells at great length on the same branch of culture. Napoleon Bonaparte has left his testimony that religion is the foundation of education. Daniel Webster has said that the Christian religion is " of the essence, the vitality of useful instruction." " Hence, since the introduction of Christianity, it has been the duty, as it has been the effort of the great and good, to sanctify human knowledge, to bring it to the font and baptize learning into Christianity, to gather up all its productions, its earliest and its latest, its blossoms and its fruits, and lay them all upon the altar of religion and virtue." And mark the reverence and devoutness of the greatest minds in scientific investigations. Listen to Kepler: "I give thee thanks, Lord and Creator, that thou hast given me delight in thy creation, and I have exulted in the work of thy hands. I have revealed to mankind the glory of thy works, as far as my limited mind could take in that infinite glory." "If I have given forth anything that is unworthy of thee, or if I have sought my own fame, wilt thou, gracious and merciful, forgive me." Hear Linnæus in his researches among the plants: "*Deum sempiternum, omniscium, omnipotentem, a tergo transeuntem, vidi, et obstupui.*" Hear Lord Bacon, joining this choir of kingly worshippers: "Thou, therefore, father, who gavest the visible light as the first fruits of the creation, and at the comple-

3

tion of thy works didst inspire the countenance of
man with intellectual light, guard and direct this work,
which proceeding from thy bounty, seeks in return
thy glory." "If we labor in thy works, thou wilt
make us partakers of thy vision and of thy Sabbath.
We pray that this mind may abide in us; and that
by our hands and the hands of others to whom thou
shalt impart the same mind, thou wilt be pleased to
endow with new gifts the family of man."

We are in sympathy, then, with the great masters
of learning, as well as with Jesus and the apostles, when
we demand that education aim pre-eminently to cultivate the moral and spiritual side of man's being, and
to establish, strengthen and settle the pupil in the
principles and practice of Christian character.

We meet, indeed, a difficulty growing out of the
multiplicity of denominations. The difficulty is safely
met in the common school, by leaving the distinctive
religious instruction to the parents. But it cannot be
met in the same way at college, for, the pupils being
away from home, it would deprive them of religious
instruction during the four most formative years of life.
To the innumerable evils arising from sectarian jeal-
ousy we must not add this more fatal than all, of
making college education unchristian through fear lest
in teaching Christianity, we seem to teach sectarianism. That would be to sacrifice our own sons to the
demon. That could be justified only by a sectarianism
so intense that it would leave the educated intellect of

the country unchristian rather than have it Christian
in any sect not our own. The difficulty has been met
by a common consent that every college have a denominational character in the sense that its religious
instruction accord with some one denomination. In
this sense Harvard, Brown, Amherst, Yale, and in fact
every college in N. England, and almost every one in
the United States, is denominational. In the same
sense and no other Bowdoin has always had a denominational character. That character has been the
same from the beginning. I know no desire or purpose in any quarter to make its character in this respect in the future any other than it has always been
in the past. But while every college is in this sense
denominational, no college ought to be sectarian, or
be made an engine for propagating sectarian narrowness and animosity. The tendency of high culture is
always to enlarge the views, to liberalize the feelings,
to purge away partizan bias, passion and prejudice.
A college would be perverted from the high ends of
liberal education, to say nothing of Christian culture,
if made an engine of sectarian zeal or political fac-
tion. Especially at this time, when the united energies of all Christians are needed to counteract the
powerful influences undermining all Christian faith,
and when the whole Christian community is yearning
for union and co-operation, the young must be educated to the large-heartedness as well as to the devoted-
ness and earnestness of Christian love. The instruc-

tion should be, as President Woolsey in his Inaugural expressed his views of religious instruction at Yale, in "a theology so liberal—if that might be—as not to pertain to the party but to universal Christianity, and so majestic in its outline as to commend itself to the consciousness and make it own the presence of God."

I add, in opposition to the current opinion, that the moral and religious interests of a young man are probably safer in college than in any other situation in which young men are congregated away from home. I make this assertion after long observation, and I am sure that facts sustain it. It has been estimated—I know not with what correctness—that one in four of the young men who go into business in the cities, come to ruin financially and morally. Compare a New England college with an equal number of young men in the shops and stores of any street of a city, you will find in college less of the mean vices of pilfering and lying, less of nightly revels and degrading sensuality; you will find a smaller proportion who, virtuous at coming, become morally corrupted; and a larger proportion whose moral character is improved, who rise to a higher sense of honor, who are rescued from corruption to which before entering they had been tending, or who are renovated to Christian faith and love.

Training, then, is the first and dominant design of collegiate education; training that produces the happiest development of the physical, intellectual and moral powers.

The second design is to impart knowledge. A well arranged college course will impart the largest amount of useful knowledge possible in securing the most complete mental discipline.

But the value of the college course in this respect does not consist so much in the amount of knowledge as in its quality.

Observe, first, that the student is so far initiated into the various great spheres of learning as to awaken an interest in them and a desire to prosecute them further. Whatever his subsequent profession, he will be in sympathy with all literature and science, will be an intelligent and interested observer of the progress of thought and discovery, and a man of large and liberal culture.

Observe, secondly, that the college has given him a knowledge of principles and methods, rather than of details. And one principle is worth a thousand facts; and a method is a key to science.

Observe, next, that the knowledge acquired is scientific rather than popular, and this gives the student a solid basis for enlarging his knowledge of applications and results.

Observe, also, that the student has acquired the knowledge and use of languages and of mathematics which are instruments of investigation available in all his subsequent life.

When the quality of the knowledge acquired in college is appreciated, it will be evident that this second part of the work accomplished is of vast consequence.

III. *Methods of realizing the idea of collegiate education.*
First, I must speak of government and discipline.

No community can prosper without the maintenance of order by the enforcement of law. Yet all admit that the maintenance of discipline is the one great difficulty in administering a college. In the recent discussions respecting reform in Harvard university, it has been intimated that the result of discipline there has been to throw the students and faculty into antagonism as hostile parties in perpetual feud. It has even been suggested that the attempt to maintain college government be abandoned as impracticable, and the students be left amenable only to the civil law. The example of the European universities is not to be appealed to in support of this, since they correspond to our professional schools rather than to our colleges. Certainly the New England mind will not consent to this in collegiate education. The difficulty probably originates less in the administration of college government than in the state of society, the decay of family government, the neglect to cultivate subordination and respectfulness in the young, and the forgetfulness of the maxim that no one knows how to command till he has first learned to obey. Colleges are not to be blamed for failing to accomplish results which the constant and irresistible influences of society render impossible.

/

I do not intend to discuss this subject in full. I propose merely to call attention to one aspect of it, which has not received due attention from American educators. ·

There are two principles, not contradictory but complements of each other, opposite poles of truth, both necessary to the complete circuit of thought on the subject. Held separately they lead to two systems of educational discipline, each erroneous because expressing only a half truth. I may best exhibit them by historical instances.

The first is exemplified in the education given by the Jesuits to those who were trained for the service of the order. This was almost exclusively discipline, severe and protracted exercises through which the pupil was required to pass, not to store his mind with knowledge, or to train him to think, reason and speak, but to discipline him to subordination, to the submission of his will without question to his superiors, to entire consecration to the interests of the order, to the abandonment of ease, sloth, pleasure and luxury, and to contempt of hardship, poverty, toil, suffering and death in its service. Here was a system which deliberately imposed the severest artificial restraints and hardships on the pupils on purpose to train them to endure hardness. The success of this training the history of Jesuit missions demonstrates.

The other principle in its exclusive application is exemplified in the account which Montaigne gives of his own education. His father, he tells us, "had been advised to make me relish science and duty by an unforced will and of my own voluntary motion, and to educate my soul in all liberty and delight without any severity or constraint." Accordingly to save him from the drudgery of learning, his attendants spoke only Latin, that he might acquire the language as a vernacular. "As to Greek, of which I have but little smattering, my father also designed to have taught it me by art, but in a new way and as a sort of sport; tossing out declensions to and fro, after the manner of those who by certain games at tables and chess learn geometry and arithmetic." The servants were forbidden to awake him in the morning, but a musician was provided to play soft music as he waked, that his mind might be serene when he arose. "By which example," he says, "you may judge of the rest." Hence resulted his marked disinclination to encounter toil or hardship, the busy idleness of his whole life, and his incapacity to appreciate the battle of human life against ignorance and wickedness.

The latter is becoming the type of modern education. Says Mr. Youmans: "The free and healthy exercise of the faculties is so pleasurable as universally to be spoken of as play. Who then, has a right to turn it into dreary and repulsive work? The love of enjoyment is the deepest and most powerful impulse of our nature, and the educational system which does not recognize and build upon it, violates the highest claim of that nature." Most true; and yet but a half truth. For life is not play, but work. It cannot be made all pleasurable, but must involve for the accomplishment of its high ends painful self-denial, sacrifice and toil. No education fits a man for real life which does not train him to endure hardness, to scorn idleness, enervation and luxury, to forego ease and indulgence, to accept toil for the accomplishment of high ends. The command to self-denial has never been repealed; the acceptance of it can never cease to be the condition of entering into life.

The error of the Mediæval education was that it was ascetic in the bad sense which that word has acquired. But there is a proper ΑΣΚΗΣΙΣ an "exercising" of the soul in conquering difficulties, bearing restraints, enduring hardness and loss, sacrificing pleasure and drudging through tasks for high ends, without which the soul can never be master of its highest strength nor realize its highest greatness. All who have achieved the most have exhibited this power— witness the ancient Romans, the Saracens, the Puritans.

Every right system of education must provide this true ASKESIS, this exercise and discipline which shall train the man to simplicity of character, purity and elevation of desires, and earnestness of purpose. It must produce men who live to achieve, not to enjoy; whose joy is in work, not in indulgence. Otherwise education produces only weaklings, whose only concern is their own comfort; whose highest end in life

4

is to have a good time; Sybarites at last who kill the cocks that their slumber may not be disturbed, and banish the smiths because they cannot endure the noise, and who cannot sleep at night if the rose leaves lie too thick on them. And this ASKESIS is as indispensable today as ever in all right training.

How then is it to be secured? Not by abandoning discipline, but by clearing it from its errors. The ascetic training of the Jesuit aimed to regulate thought and to make the mind and will submissive to authority. Our ASKESIS must aim to make a man a thinker, independent in thought and action, but reverently submissive to truth and right; and in obedience thereto freely consecrated to God in the service of man. The mediæval asceticism was imposed by authority; ours must be accepted freely through interest in the noblest ends. The ancient asceticism imposed artificial restraints, privations and sufferings for the purpose of training men to hardness; ours must not be artificial but natural, accordant with the discipline which life itself imposes on every man; rejoicing in every gift of God as good, and accepting the discipline simply as incidental to the achievements on which the heart is bent. In real life nothing is offered gratis. Nature sells, and always at the value price. The discipline of a college should be simply the conformity of the college to this great law of nature and of life.

Therefore there should be no artificial regulations creating offences which but for the rules would not

have been offences. Where numbers are prosecuting
studies together there must necessarily be fixed hours
for college exercises, and fixed hours of study when,
for the common convenience, the colleges and grounds
shall be quiet and studies may be prosecuted without
interruption. Beyond this the young man in college
should be held to the same law which governs all human life; he must be held to truthfulness, sincerity,
justice, kindness, honor, integrity, in action and spirit;
to gentlemanliness and courtesy; to diligence and
energy in study and the concentration of all his powers
on gaining that high education which is the immediate
object of the college life. For that end he must be
content to forego ease and indulgence and to work
with all his might. All requirements of constant and
punctual attendance, all assignment of studies easy or
hard, all stimulus and pressure to bring out his energies and make him accomplish the utmost consistent
with health, he must accept, not as the arbitrary regulation of college, but simply as the enforcement in college of the great law of nature and of life that value
must be paid for; that the good of life is gained only
by toil and self-denial. "Buy the truth."

If any student is persistently idle, if he falls into
dissipation or other vice, if he habitually disturbs
the quiet and order of the college, if he violates the
rights of his fellow students or trespasses on the property or peace of the community, and will not heed
admonition, he must be dismissed. Thus the same

laws of propriety and virtue rule in college which rule in society at large; the law which in college requires punctuality, self-restraint, diligence and energy, is the law which requires the same in actual life. Thus the whole college course will be a constant appeal to all the best sentiments of the heart, and a constant training to self-government; and to self-denying and energetic work. And he who has not acquired this capacity must be in society a useless thing; and when he dies nobody will mourn that the earth is relieved of the burden of his support.

The course of study has also been under discussion, and great changes have been demanded.

The demand that increased attention be given to the natural sciences is reasonable. The recent expansion of knowledge in this direction has been so great, that a collegiate education cannot be complete, nor adapted to the times, which does not introduce the student to these sciences. They provide also a peculiar intellectual discipline; they train the powers of observation, of discrimination and classification; they educate in inductive reasoning; they hold the mind rigorously to facts; they restrain, or at least ought to restrain the tendency to fanciful speculation and theorising. Although I am constrained to say that if seeking through all the history of speculation for the most striking instance of the inverted pyramid, the broadest theory on the smallest apex of fact, I should find it among the shifting scientific theories of cosmology and paleontology. It may be added, that the basis of mathematics which underlies many of these studies necessitates in them a mathematical discipline. Therefore aside from the knowledge acquired, these studies are important to supplement other studies in securing a complete and harmonious intellectual discipline.

I heartily agree with the modern demand for a more extended course in natural science. And yet I object to it, as actually urged, that it is but a half truth, and as such tends to evil. There are three great spheres of human thought, Nature, Man, and God. My objection to the demand under consideration is that in effect it acknowledges only the first of these and allows no proper proportion of attention to the other two. Thus it tends always to the fatal doctrine that the knowledge of matter and of physical force is the only knowledge useful or possible to man.

First, in claiming that the knowledge of these branches is pre-eminently useful knowledge, an inadequate idea of utility is involved. If that only is useful which aids in feeding, clothing and sheltering man, then indeed the knowledge of natural science is the only useful knowledge; then all useful knowledge may be included under the German designation *Brodwissenschaft*, which may be translated, "Bread and butter science"; and the tendency to materialism becomes inevitable and irresistible.

But the highest product of the earth is not corn

and cotton, but man. The highest end of education is to elevate and develop man. The true utility consists in promoting this high end.

Even if we give the widest scope to the common argument from the utility of the natural sciences, it acknowledges as useful only that which supplies existing human wants, and overlooks the prior necessity of so developing the man that he may have wants large, manifold, pure and elevated, which discovery and invention may meet. This is the prime and fundamental utility.

In truth the first named utility is subordinate to and dependent on this second and true utility. Of what use to multiply inventions and facilities of production while man is capable only of the hideous pleasures of savage life? The wants of the savage are so few and so gross, his desires are so brutish and his pleasures so disgusting, that knowledge and art have but the most limited scope in which they can minister to his wants. The man himself must first be developed. The civilized man is many times more a man than the savage. We say he has more wants. That is because he is more developed; he has become many sided; his tastes have been purified; his desires have been multiplied and elevated; the sources of interest and avenues of enjoyment have become manifold more numerous. Nature touches him at a thousand-fold more points than the savage, and can give him a thousand-fold more and better blessings. Therefore the prime necessity and highest utility is the development of the man.

The same argument may be drawn from a comparison of civilized men. How limited the scope in which knowledge and art could have been useful to Nero, who, with the resources of the Roman Empire at his sole command to suck it dry as a man sucks an orange, was yet capable of obtaining from all the riches of the world only the sordid pleasures of intemperance and the horrid pleasures of cruelty. Even in civilization, therefore, the degree to which knowledge can be useful to a man, depends on the development and culture of the man; as the degree to which sunshine and rain can bless a soil depends on the richness and culture of the soil.

The history of science and art in all ages presents facts in confirmation. It is true of many modern inventions and discoveries that they had been found out by some thinker generations before they came into use, but dropped into oblivion again because society was not sufficiently advanced, that is, man was not sufficiently developed to need or to use them. From the days of Archimedes until now, discoveries and inventions have been falling on society and perishing without fruit, like seed incapable of germinating, and obliged to perish, because thrown upon a rock.

Therefore, I repeat, the highest utility consists in the development of man himself. We may say it is the one fundamental utility; because it is only as this development is realized that science and art find scope to be useful to man.

If so, then the natural sciences have no exclusive or even pre-eminent claim to be useful knowledge, or to be the exclusive or even the pre-eminent studies in education. If man is the highest product of the earth, if his development is the grandest end, then the study of man must be equal in dignity and importance to the study of that which merely ministers to his existing wants : and we may re-assert in this century what was a truism in the last; "The proper study of mankind is man." On the ground of utility alone I claim the higher place for the study of man himself; those studies fitly called "the humanities" ; the great courses of human thought; the questions which have occupied the human mind ; the products of human genius; the progress and characteristics of civilization; the conditions and laws of individual action and of the constitution and welfare of society.

And if so, then the knowledge of human languages and literature is pre-eminently useful knowledge; for it is pre-eminently the knowledge of man. Comparative Philology is a sort of geology of human thought. In the study of languages the student digs through the strata in which the opinions, the religion, the politics, the social customs of the past have been deposited. Single words are petrified thoughts, fossils perpetuating some peculiar formation in the life of a distant age. Why is not this knowledge as useful as the knowledge of the deposition of sand and gravel in the ages before human history began? Literature is the consummate flower and fruit of the human mind, the product of the greatest geniuses which have made the history of the race illustrious. In these studies, also, a student best masters his own language, and acquires the power of expressing his own thoughts.

The language and literature of Greece and Rome are by universal consent among the most important. In them we come in contact with the human mind in its most formative and influential periods. The civilization of Greece and Rome have been determinant forces in the formation of our modern civilization; and with the civilization of the Hebrews, fused together under the power of Christianity mightier than all three, still penetrate our civilization as they do our language, with elements of abiding power. What a blank would be made in the mind of any highly educated person, if there were struck out at a dash all the knowledge, the culture, the refinement and enlargement of thought, the intellectual strength acquired from contact with the Greek and Roman mind.

Herbert Spencer objects, I know, that the dead facts of human history are useless. I reply, that all facts are useless, except as their significance is seen through their relation to some principle, law or end. They lie like heaps of broken granite, mere rubbish, till the mind of the architect constructs them into a temple; till the Orphic music of a master thought makes them move and range themselves harmoniously in the grand and beautiful whole. So the facts of meteorology lie accumulated in huge volumes of recorded observations, meaningless as the incongruous images of Nebuchadnezzar's dream, waiting the Daniel who shall tell us their significance. But this is no more true of the facts of human than of natural history. A dead man is no more dead than a dead dog. If we must compare the value of mere facts, why is not the knowledge that Cæsar crossed the Rubicon as useful as the knowledge of the average weight of the human brain? The knowledge of the migrations of men and the founding of empires as useful as the knowledge of the movements of great glaciers in an immeasurably distant geological epoch? Why are we not as much benefited by knowing the names of Aristides and Socrates, of Cato and Brutus, as by learning to call a certain shell fish no longer a clam, but a *Mya Arenaria*? And why is not a knowledge of mythology, which Spencer especially ridicules, being the knowledge of the action of the human mind on the great subject of religion, as capable of use as the knowledge of the monstrous shapes and names of Pentacrinite, Ichthyosaurus, Megalosaurus, and all the " chimæras dire " of geology?

I accept, then, the test of utility. I agree with Milton,

> " That not to know at large of things remote
> From use, obscure and subtle ; but to know
> That which before us lies in daily life,.
> Is the prime wisdom."

Yet I insist that man is himself the highest product of the earth; that his development is the highest end of education; that the utility which consists in satisfying existing wants is inferior and subordinate to the prime utility which consists in developing, purifying and ennobling the man; and that in any view of the subject a knowledge of the languages, history and literature of man is at least as useful as a knowledge of nature.

It may be argued in reply that even for the highest end of education, natural science is the more effective. Admitting that the utility of knowledge is to be tested, not merely by its bearing on the supply of existing wants, but on the development, purification and ennobling of man, it may be contended that the knowledge of nature is still pre-eminently the useful knowledge. But this admission changes the whole question; it rectifies the one-sided and inadequate view of utility, which constitutes a fallacy in the argument and necessitates a tendency to materialism. When the question is thus put, the same correct test of utility being appealed to on each side, the respective claims of the different departments of knowledge can be adjudicated. I will only throw out a single thought bearing on this adjudication. The facts of history disprove Comte's theory that the progress of the human mind has always been by successive steps from Theology to Metaphysics and thence to Natural Science; for these have always been co-existent factors of civilization. But history does demonstrate that in the earlier periods of civilization, romance and poetry, æsthetics and literature, rhetoric, logic, and language, ethics and politics, metaphysics and theology, were much larger factors in the education of the race than natural science; and that the same continued to be the fact up to the most recent centuries. And the civilization which produced Homer and Virgil, Socrates, Plato, and Aristotle, Pericles, and Julius Cæsar, has something to say for itself as to its capacity to develop man. Confessedly the natural sciences have become prominent factors in the education of the race only in the last period of its progress. Even during the last two centuries as much of human thought has been expended on the study of man and God as on the study of nature; education in the schools has continued to this day to be principally in those studies; and the most eminent naturalists owe their own discipline and training first to them.

Now let it be observed that education must guide the development of every child from the incapacity, ignorance and rudeness of barbarism up to the highest civilization—each child passing through in its own progress the entire progress of the race—and it is reasonable to infer that the same order of studies by which God has educated the race will be the order most effective to educate the individual. Such in substance has been the order of educational influences which either the wisdom or the instinct of man has adopted. And until babes shall begin to be born civilized men and women, there will be no reason, even in the nineteenth century, to change substantially this order, but only to perfect and improve the details.

A second objection against the argument for a larger attention to the natural sciences is its tendency —I speak of a tendency involved, rather than of a theory avowed—to make education only a special training for a special work, and to overlook the previous general training which gives development and culture to the man. The argument constantly urged, that education from the beginning must consist in the acquisition of knowledge that is to be used in the special work of life, has force only on the premise that all education is a special training for a special work. This false theory of education is latent in the argument. Indeed, in Comte's system it is not latent. At an early age the special adaptation of the child is to be determined by a phrenological examination by state officials; thenceforward he is to be taken from his parents, and educated for that special trade or business.

To see how pernicious this error is, notice, first, that after all the broader culture of the college there are certain isolating, one-sided, narrowing influences, a certain professional smack and odor, inseparable from every special profession, trade or business; a certain incapacity, also, to appreciate the knowledge, skill, difficulties, work and worth of other pursuits. If now the training of the college be omitted, and instead, education from the beginning be a special training for a special work, these narrowing influences will be intolerably intensified. If a person is to spend life in making pins, and his entire education has consisted in acquiring the knowledge and skill necessary for that business, the result is that the man disappears, and a pin-maker alone remains. If the same theory of education be universally adopted, then in the multitude of artisans and professional drudges, we shall need Diogenes' lamp to find a man.

Here comes in sight another fatal tendency of this error. It is argued that education must be the teaching of the knowledge and skill which are to be used in the special business of life. This argument has force only on the premise that the artisan is of more consequence than the man; that the highest end of education is to produce the skill of the artisan, not the excellence of the man. Thence it follows that the product of work is of more value than the workman. Thence, in one line of inference, it follows that the workman may be sacrificed to multiply the products of his labor; all assertions of the dignity and rights of labor, of the sacredness of humanity, of inalienable rights are silenced; the door is open for the re-entry of slavery or any enforced service which promises to multiply products.

In another line of inference it follows that since the highest end is the multiplication of products, all utility lies in that direction, and the farthest scope and highest end of civilization is limited to the material.

Here we come in sight of two systems of civilization struggling already in the womb of time for the
birthright of precedence and lordship in the future—
systems contrasted long ago by Jesus—the one that
man lives by bread alone; the other, that he lives by
the word of God;—the one, which affirms with Comte
that man must abandon his claim to be the lowest of
the angels and must be content henceforth to rank as
the highest of the beasts; the other, which acknowledges him as spiritual and immortal, in the image of
God;—the one, which sees utility only in the multiplication of products, and, sinking the man in the artisan, appoints him to moil and fatten "where wealth
accumulates and men decay"; the other, which subor-
dinates all to man's intellectual, æsthetic, social and
spiritual culture;—the one, which with Lord Bacon
recognizes man in his highest exaltation as no more
than the minister and interpreter, that is, the servant
and student of nature; the other, which with Kepler
recognizes the student and interpreter of nature as
also the student and interpreter of the divine mind,
reading God's thoughts after him, and, with the Bible,
recognizes man not as the servant but the Lord of nature, appointed to possess its resources and to compel
the service of its forces;—the one, which explains all
human progress as the result of physical forces, developing according to their necessary law; the other,
which regards it as the result of spiritual energies
originating in God's love, expressing the action of his

grace, establishing on earth a kingdom of righteous-
ness and peace, renovating the earth by and for man,
and installing him in that lordship over nature for
which he was created.

I insist that in the conflict of civilizations, all right
education must be unmistakably and emphatically pro-
nounced on the side of the latter against the former.
I object to the plea for the natural sciences and against
the humanities in education that so often there are
arguments which have no validity and appeals which
have no force, except by admitting as premises princi-
ciples which legitimately lead to a materialistic civilization.

I need not draw on my own imagination to depict
this type of civilization; for Comte has fully delineated
it. For example, he insists that the stellar astronomy,
as the investigation of binary stars, ought not to be
studied because it is not available for practical use—
making of no account the inextinguishable interest of
the soul in truth for its own sake, and all the higher
uses of such investigations in quickening the imagination, elevating the thoughts, and enlarging our ideas
of the glory of the universe and of God. In that
state of society which Comte depicts as the highest
civilization, the man is educated to be an artisan and is
lost in the artisan; he is of less value than his products, and, if it is needful, is to be sacrificed to multiply them; he is the tool of the state, having no rights
but only owing duties; the modern doctrines of hu-

man rights and civil liberty are ridiculous errors; the
State is a hierarchy of *savans*, determining despotically
every person's business, regulating the minutiæ of con-
duct, and like the Inquisition, carrying its dictation
and espionage into the sphere of opinion and con-
science and into all the privacy of life; love is regulated by the State; the glow of passion and the freedom of impulse are suppressed, nobleness of character
and heroism of action are made impossible; indi-
viduality is lost in the monotony of a universal and
regulated productiveness; and even the creation of
value and the acquisition of property, while it is the
highest end of life, is yet restrained from kindling passion or awakening desire. This is his boasted *autruism*
with which he caricatures Christian love—in name
that a man lives for others—in reality that he is the
tool of the State for the production of value. In such
a civilization Mother Goose and Fairy tales must give
place to useful knowledge in the nursery. All the romance of life, which is like the bloom on the plum
and the down on the peach, must be rubbed off; and
the spring, freedom and variety of life give place to
calculating prudence and frigid regulation. J. S. Mill
himself takes note of this already discernible tendency.
He says, "The chivalrous spirit has nowadays almost
disappeared from our books of education. For the
first time in history the young of both sexes are growing up unromantic." There results at last an inca-

6

pacity even to comprehend the loftier enthusiasm and the deeper springs of human action; as Voltaire could account for the Protestant Reformation only as the result of a quarrel between the Augustinian and Dominican monks. This is the vision of the good time coming, according to the gospel of the Positive Philosophy. And when it has fully come, we may expect the women to dispense with useless ornaments and have interest tables printed on their aprons; and then may be realized, in accordance with what Herbert Spencer urges, the substitution in the course of study for young men in college of a treatise on hygiene instead of Greek, and a treatise on the rearing of children instead of Latin.

I do not speak of these tendencies as belonging to the study of the natural sciences; but as indicated and involved in the current arguments for the substitution of this study for that of Latin and Greek and of the " humanities " in general.

On the contrary I insist that these false arguments do injustice to these sciences and place them in a false position. I advocate increased attention to these sciences in college, not merely because they are useful in reference to the supply of material wants, nor because they secure a peculiar and necessary kind of intellectual discipline, but also because they enlarge the range of thought, awaken a new and higher interest in nature, and have utility in its highest sense in pro-

moting the culture and development of man and the.
best progress of society. The Atlantic cable does not
merely transmit the quotations of the markets, but in it

" The hands of human brotherhood
Are clasped beneath the sea."

While in ancient civilization labor was servile, and the
only scope for honorable ambition was in politics or
war, modern discoveries and inventions have facilitated
labor and made it honorable, have exalted private business into a public service, have given scope in industrial
pursuits to the highest enterprise and genius, and are
compelling the nations to feel a common interest as
members of the one common family of man.

Moreover if languages, literature and philosophy
give to the student the thoughts of man, in natural
science, as Kepler said and as Agassiz teaches, we read
the thoughts of God.

It must be added that the physical sciences in their
latest investigations have themselves become metaphysical. The question, ".What is force?" belongs at once
to physics and to metaphysics. In the doctrine of the
correlation and co-ordination of forces, physical science
becomes profoundly metaphysical. When science demonstrates that all force is one, variously transmuted ;
that heat, light and electricity are transmuted motion
and may be transmuted back into motion, it therein
equally demonstrates that physical science itself is
transmuted metaphysics and may be transmuted back

into metaphysics, and even into theology. Herbert Spencer himself teaches that science brings us in sight of a force absolute, eternal and inexhaustible. Thus the last word of physical science is the first word of theology.

The irresistible conclusion is that the healthy and complete course of college study, whether we regard mental discipline or useful knowledge, is that which touches in due proportion the three great subjects of human thought, Nature, Man, and God.

Alumni and friends of Bowdoin College, I have now set before you my views of the necessity, the idea and the methods of collegiate education. It will be my aim to meet these necessities and to realize this ideal. It is to the honor of the State that a college with these high aims was founded so early in what was then the Province of Maine. Its history has been one which has been an honor to the State. Its graduates have been active and influential in all departments of life. No New England college can show among its alumni a larger proportion of men distinguished in literature and science, and in professional, political and military life. In its course of study it has always aimed at the substantial rather than the showy, at the real rather than the factitious. It has always been slow to adopt novelties, and yet in repeated instances has taken the lead in introducing changes which time and the general concurrence of the colleges have demonstrated to be improvements. While in the future as in the past we shall not make haste in innovations, we shall strive to keep abreast of the progress of society, and to adopt all the improvements which that progress demands and by which it can be wisely promoted. ˙ I am sure every alumnus of the college has reason to be proud of his Alma Mater for her record in the past. And I trust that they and all friends of sound learning will give their influence and aid to make her record still brighter in the future ; that while we joyfully urge forward the development of the resources of the State and multiply our railroads, our mills and the product of our farms, we may in the same proportion increase our interest in education, and enlarge the resources of this old and honored institution.